SWANSEA SINCE 1900

1. Craddock Street at the turn of the century.

NIGEL ARTHUR

First published 1988 by

Archive Publications Ltd
Carrington Business Park
Urmston
Manchester

in association with the

South Wales Evening Post
P O Box 14
Adelaide Street
Swansea

Printed and bound in the United Kingdom
by
Netherwood Dalton Ltd., Huddersfield.

ISBN: 0-948946-20-2

2. Department of Transport's Driver and Vehicle Licensing Centre at Morriston, Swansea.

Contents

Introduction and Acknowledgements

The idea behind this volume is to reflect on Swansea's development for better or for worse, firstly as a town then as a city, since the end of the last century through the medium of photography. The majority of these photographs were taken by staff photographers at the *South Wales Evening Post* and to them I am especially grateful. The rest of the photographs came from a wide variety of sources and I hope I have duly acknowledged everyone who contributed. I would like to thank all the people and organisations who helped me compile this book. I would like to thank my parents, my wife and my friends for their support and encouragement. Thanks to Clive Hardy and to Henry Hochland and the Archive Publications team; Peter Lloyd and Andy Cox; Gareth Mills for help with the Swansea Docks section; Doug Jones of Associated British Ports, South Wales Group Office, Bute Docks, Cardiff; Dr J R Alban and Gwyn Davies of the City Archives Office, the Guildhall, Swansea; Swansea City Council; Betty Nelmes and General Gabb of Swansea Museum (Royal Institution of South Wales); Neil Hadkiss, Des Cannon and Jackie Haynes for all their help at the *South Wales Evening Post;* Swansea Central Library, Alexandra Road; The Glynn Vivian Art Gallery, Alexandra Road; and especially to David Rowe, Brenda Bloxam and to all the artists who kindly loaned their work to us from the Attic Gallery, Wind Street, Swansea.

3. A panoramic view of Port Talbot steelworks.

Old Swansea

4. High Street, Swansea, at the turn of the century.

5. High Street, Swansea, in 1915.

6. Note how the tramtracks are laid to allow a passing loop in a confined space.

HIGH STREET (No. 3), SWANSEA.

7. The now nomore Peoples Bioscope Palace, High Street.

8. View south along Castle Street in the 1930s. Note Ben Evans store in the centre background.

9. Swansea was heavily bombed on three consecutive nights in February 1941. This view of Ben Evans store in Castle Street shows the demolition teams beginning the awesome task of clearing up the mess.

10. *Opposite top:* Late nineteenth century view of Walter Road. Note absence of tramlines.

11. *Opposite bottom:* Walter Road in the early 1900s.

12. Oxford Street in the early 1920s.

13 & 14. Oxford Street in the early 1900s.

15. Oxford Street c1921

16. A street tramcar approaches the junction of Oxford Street and Dilwyn Street sometime in the late 1920s or early 1930s. Street tramcars were taken out of service in 1936.

17. Aerial view of the centre of Swansea taken in 1928.

18. Central Swansea as it appeared in 1950. A modified street plan has already been started with the creation of the Kingsway out of Gower Street and part of St Helen's Road.

19. Swansea Hospital at the turn of the century.

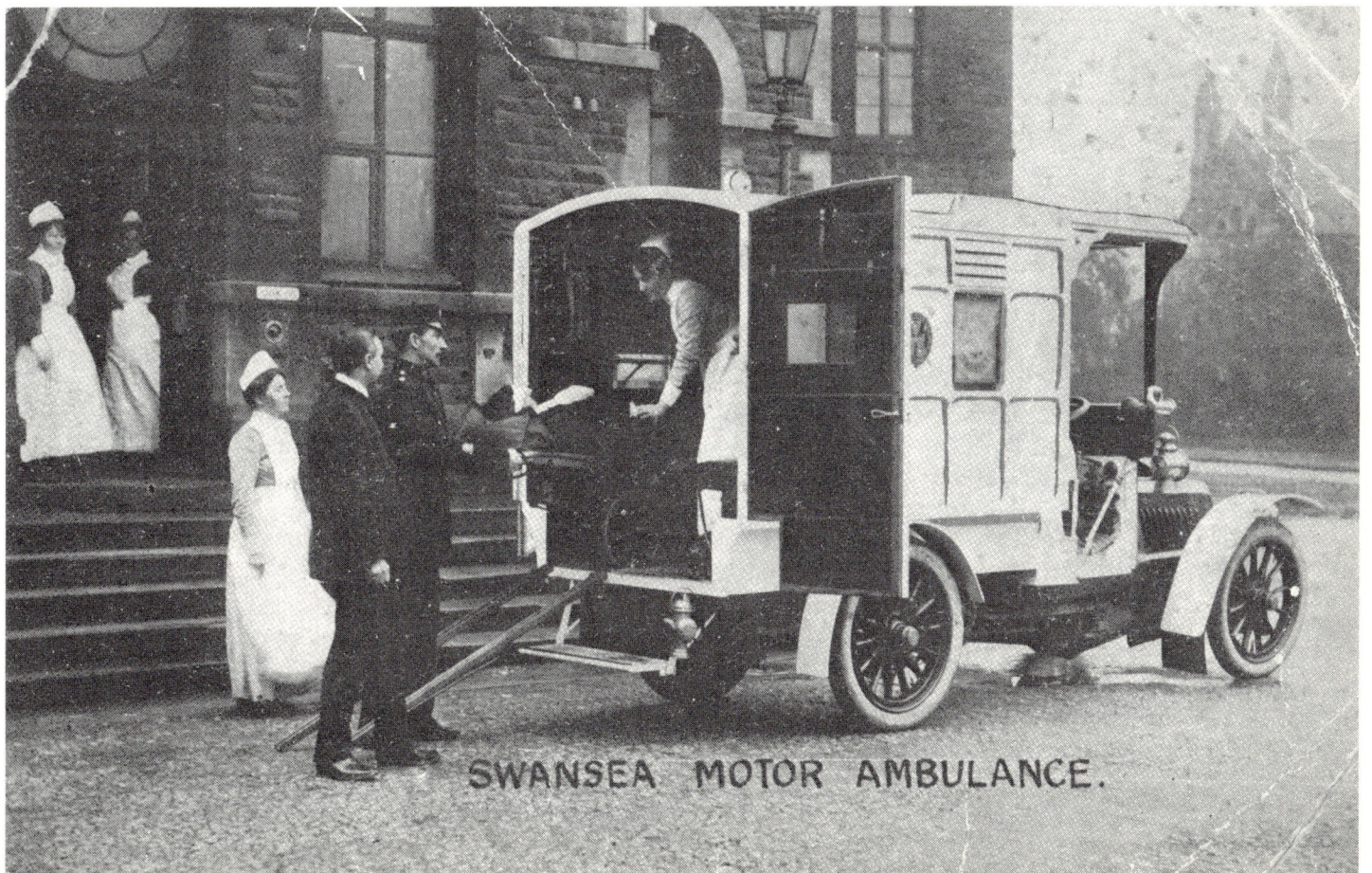

SWANSEA MOTOR AMBULANCE.

20. The first motor ambulance at Swansea Hospital c1914.

21. Postcard of Langland Bay, Mumbles, pre-World War One.

22. Sun seekers and bathing machines.

23. Between the wars but prior to the electrification of the Mumbles Railway.

Mumbles Railway 1804-1960

24. Ladies on bicycles attempt to outdo the Mumbles Train for speed c1910.

25. Typical of the turn out on a hot summer Sunday's trip to Mumbles. Travellers could be served alcoholic beverages in pubs on a Sunday, and drunkeness, swearing and brawling was not unknown, especially amongst young girls!

6. Mumbles train halted at Oystermouth tation in the early 1900s.

TRAIN AT OYSTERMOUTH STATION, MUMBLES

27. The paddle-steamer *Brighton* (593 tons) lies moored to Mumbles Pier in 1910. Owned by Pockett's Bristol Channel Steam Packet Company, the *Brighton* undertook pleasure trips to Ilfracombe until requisitioned by the Admiralty for war service. She sailed to Gallipoli in 1915.

28. *centre left:* Approaching Mumbles.

29. *centre right:* Steam locomotive *Swansea* in the 1920s.

30. *left:* A replica constructed in 1954 to mark the 150th Anniversary celebrations of the creation of the Swansea to Mumbles Railway. This is how people would have travelled in 1820.

31. *opposite page:* A van leaving St Helen's Goods Yard was crushed by a passing train on 6 September 1957. Each tramcar weighed 26 tons unladen and the van had been struck by a moving object weighing at least 50 tons. The electric tramcars were introduced in 1929 replacing the old steam engines, and were built by Brush Electrical Engineering Co of Loughborough.

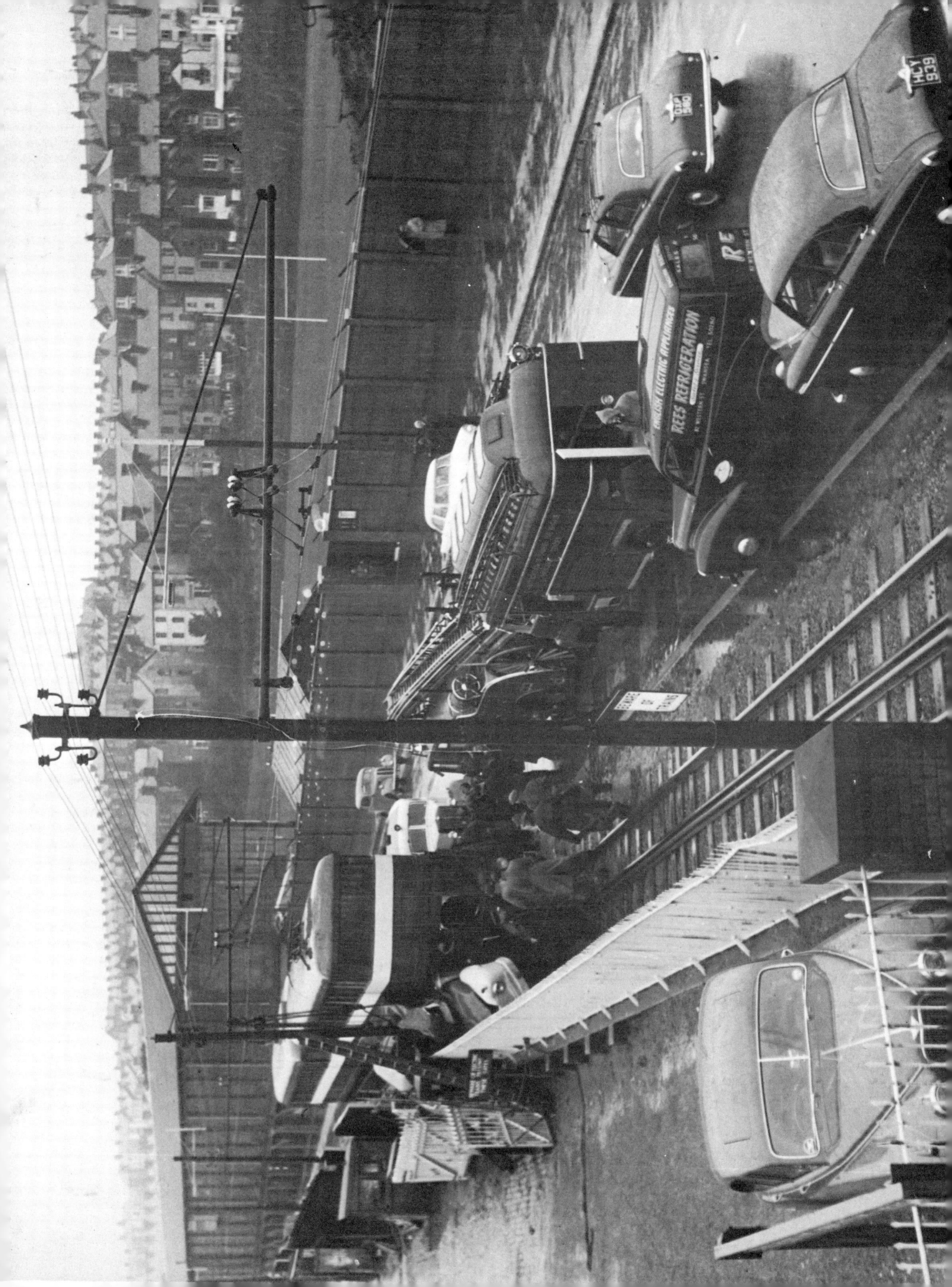

32 & 33. The end is nigh for the Mumbles Railway, January 1960.

34 - 36. Oiling the points for the last time, 5 January 1960. On 5 January 1960 a last ceremonial train ran between Swansea and Mumbles.

37 & 38. It's smiles for the *South Wales Evening Post* photographer as the last train prepares to leave. *below:* The last train heads back towards Swansea.

39. Only two days after the closure the demolition was already well advanced, 7 January 1960.

OYSTERMOUTH

40 & 41. Something was saved from the Mumbles Railway before everything was swept away. The cab was cut from Tramcar No 7 at Ashleigh Road and completely restored and is now preserved for posterity in Swansea's Industrial and Maritime Museum where it is an evocative reminder of an age now past ... alas.

Transport
and
Travel

42. 5080 *Defiant* with the 10.48am Swansea to Paddington, 20 January 1949. Photograph by Huw Daniel.

43. 5052 *Earl of Radnor* with Meurig Davies (Tube Cleaner) on the footplate, Landore, Swansea, August 1949. Photograph by Huw Daniel.

44. The old meets the new at Swansea's High Street Station in 1987.

45. The Swansea to London route was one of the first to operate the new High Speed Inter-City 125's. The HST class 253 came into service on BR Western Region on 4 October 1976.

46. The last train pulls out of Swansea's Victoria Station before its closure in the early 1960s.

47. Swansea's High Street Station in the 1970s. Note the cost of the fares to London advertised above the entrance.

49. The Grand Hotel at High Street Station.

48. High Street Station on a bleak January day, 1987.

50. High Street Station in 1988. Note the price of the fare advertised in this photograph!

51. Open balcony tramcar No. 33 clatters along Oxford Street on the Brynmill service. The tramway system was abandoned in 1936 - a much lamented decision.

52. Swansea Improvements & Tramways Co enclosed balcony car No 8 poses for the camera of Jack Thomas.

53. Early motor-bus of the South Wales Transport Co. The small bus at left was used for publicity purposes and not necessarily for going under bridges with low clearances.

54. November 1987. City centre buses at work.

55. De Havilland DH114 Heron 1B of Morton Air Services Ltd at Fairwood Common aerodrome in the early 1960s. Note the fixed undercarriage of the early Herons.

56. Swansea Airport on Fairwood Common in July 1983. The development of Swansea Airport has meant and still means a great deal of work and initiative 'but we are confident that to maintain and develop it is a very sound long-term policy' Councillor Percy Morris, 1st January 1960. Very little remains now of its wartime heritage to remind us that during Swansea's last air raid on 16/17 February 1943, Fairwood's nightfighers shot down three German bombers and probably two others in one night's hectic action.

57. British Steel Co's executive jet, a Hawker Siddeley HS 125, at Fairwood in the late 1960s.

58. Swansea Airport in the 1980s.

59. In February 1988 British Airways named a Boeing 747 *City of Swansea*. The Lord Mayor of Swansea, Councillor Alan Ayers, is seen at the ceremony.

City Centre

60. Aerial view of Swansea showing the Market, the Quadrant Centre, St Mary's Church, the Leisure Centre and Marina at South Dock in July 1983.

61. Aerial panorama of Swansea city centre in the early 1980s.

62 & 63. *Opposite page and above*: The multi-million pound Quadrant Shopping Centre takes shape in the late 1970s.

64. The southern aspect of the Quadrant Centre with its associated multi-storey car park.

65. Quadrant Bus Station.

66. Lower Union Street leading down to the entrance to the Quadrant Centre.

67. Swansea has always been able to boast that it has an excellent shopping centre, never more so than in the 1980s with the development of the Quadrant Centre.

68. The Quadrant Centre

69 & 70. *Above and below:* Littlewoods Store on the corner of St Mary's Square.

71. St David's Shopping Centre.

72. The new Sainsbury's complex on Quay Parade.

73. Children's World on Quay Parade.

I. Swansea's Coat of Arms.

II. Swansea Docks 1969.

III. Approaching Squall, Mumbles Head by Robert Harrison (1988). *Courtesy* The Attic Gallery.

IV. Calm, Kitchen Corner (Rhossili) by Robert Harrison (1988). *Courtesy* The Attic Gallery.

V. Mumbles Pier by Mary Beresford-Williams (1982). *Courtesy* The Attic Gallery.

VI. Dickslade, Mumbles by Sarah Hopkins (1987).
Courtesy The Attic Gallery.

VII. The Pilot, Mumbles by Nicholas Penn (1984).
Courtesy The Attic Gallery.

VIII. Rotherslade Beach Huts by Sarah Hopkins (1988).
Courtesy The Attic Gallery.

IX. *King George V* at Swansea High Street Station, 1987 by R M Mumford. *Courtesy* The Attic Gallery

X. Swansea Market by Sarah Hopkins (1988). *Courtesy* The Attic Gallery.

XI. Swansea Market by Brenda Thomas (1975). *Courtesy* The Attic Gallery.

XII. Salubrious Passage by Sarah Hopkins (1988). *Courtesy* The Attic Gallery.

XIII. County Hall by R M Mumford (1986). *Courtesy* The Attic Gallery.

XIV. The Marina by Sarah Hopkins (1988). *Courtesy* The Attic Gallery.

XV. Pump House, Marina by Gareth Thomas (1988). *Courtesy* The Attic Gallery.

XVI. Swansea by John Brunsdon (1978). *Courtesy* The Attic Gallery.

XVII. The Docks from Swansea Bay by Gareth Thomas (1988). *Courtesy* The Attic Gallery.

XVIII. St. Thomas, Swansea by Sarah Hopkins (1987). *Courtesy* The Attic Gallery.

XIX. Dismantling Coal Hoists at Swansea Docks by R M Mumford (1988). *Courtesy* The Attic Gallery.

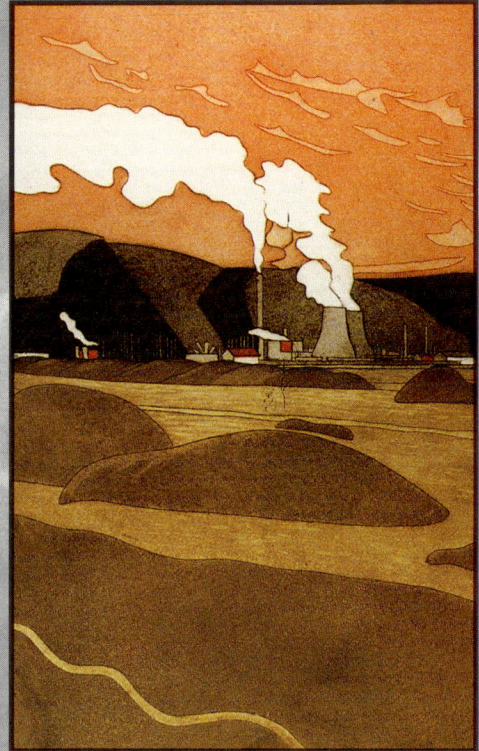

XX. Welsh Industrial Scene by John Brunsdon (1978). *Courtesy* The Attic Gallery.

XXI. RCS coil preparation line, Alcoa Manufacturing, Waunarlydd Works.

74. Castle Street in the late 1970s.

5. High Street has become a quieter place with a definite shift of the city centre away to the south upon the completion of the Quadrant Centre.

76. One of Swansea's landmarks - The Dragon Hotel. ... imposing building but one of uninspired design. Like ma... buildings of this era, it now looks sadly dated.

77. A view of Princess Way, the Kingsway and the site of *The Dragon Hotel* in the 1950s.

78. A view along Princess Way from Kingsway Roundabout c1970.

79. *Opposite page:* Photograph of Castle Gardens, Swansea Castle, Caer Street, and St Mary's Church taken from the GPO Tower. Along the Swansea Bay foreshore can be seen West Glamorgan County Hall, the Vetch Field (home of Swansea City AFC) and the Guildhall.

THE CROSS KEYS, SWANSEA

80 & 81. The oldest public house in Wales is the *Cross Keys* in Princess Way, first established in 1332.

82. Castle Gardens overlooked by the ruins of Swansea Castle and the GPO Tower.

83. Oxford Street in inclement weather, 1986.

84. Interior of Swansea Market where one can sample cockles from Llanrhidian Sands and still buy that Swansea delicacy, laverbread, made from fresh seaweed.

85. *Opposite:* Aerial view of The Kingsway and Oxford Street in the 1970s. The prominent black roof in the centre of the photograph belongs to the Odeon Cinema, which was one of the most modern cinemas in the country when built in the mid 1960s to replace the old Plaza.

86. The Kingsway during the Festive Season.

87 & 88. A blessing and a curse - the motor car endows people with tremendous mobility and range . . . when they can free themselves from the traffic which clogs our busiest roads!

89 & 90. From some angles even the GPO Tower Block can look an interesting building. It completely dominates any view of central Swansea.

91. View from the GPO/British Telecom Building looking north along The Strand towards High Sreet Station, c1986.

92. The Inland Revenue and the Land Registry buildings.

93. No, it's not Darth Vader's fortress! It's Swansea's new Land Registry.

94. High Street multi-storey car park - a design much imitated in recent public and commercial buildings in Swansea. Swansea is now a city of "car park architecture".

95. Alexandra House.

96 & 97. *left and opposite page:* High-rise flats, such as these at Dyfatty which were built in the 1960s, are now known to have been a social and environmental wrong turning.

98. Swansea Police Station on the corner of Alexandra Road and Orchard Street.

99 & 100. The Glynn Vivian Art Gallery in Alexandra Road has an important collection of Swansea China as well as a collection of paintings, sculpture, textiles and craft and design.

101 & 102. Swansea Central Library, Alexandra Road.

103 & 104. Swansea's 'grand' Grand Theatre is now one of the finest provincial theatres in the country following an extensive improvement scheme funded by the Council. The late Victorian auditorium has been preserved in all its splendour.

105. The oldest museum in Wales, Swansea Museum, was built in 1838 by the Royal Institution of South Wales. It houses collections of Natural History, Swansea and Nantgarw pottery and porcelain, archaeological pieces covering 20,000 years of local history and an exhibition of Egyptology including the mummy of the Priest Tem Hor. Dylan Thomas once remarked that it was a museum which belonged in a museum, but the Royal Institution with its "dignified classical facade" (as described by Wynford Vaughan-Thomas) has been a bastion of culture and learning since time immemorial. Long may it continue to be so!

106. Swansea Leisure Centre was opened in the late 1970s and stands on the site of the old Victoria Station. It provides numerous sporting facilities including a massive indoor swimming pool with wave machine and water shoot, squash courts and a huge indoor bowling green.

107. Almost the whole sweep of Swansea Bay is visible in this photograph with the new West Glamorgan County Council complex very much to the fore.

108. Aerial view of County Hall and the Marina development in the old South Dock, September 1986.

109. The new Crown Court on St Helen's Road across from the Guildhall, March 1988.

110. Designed by the eminent Welsh architect Sir Percy Thomas, the Guildhall was completed in 1933 and houses Swansea City Council and the Brangwyn Hall where the British Empire Panels created by Frank Brangwyn for the House of Lords are displayed. The Brangwyn Hall is Swansea's main concert hall and hosts the Swansea Music Festival each year in October.

111. The Patti Pavilion (built in 1920) in Victoria Park.

112. University College of Wales, Swansea, on Mumbles Road, with Singleton Park beyond.

Swansea Docks

113. The three masted Norwegian barque *Fritz Smith* loaded with a cargo of patent fuel in North Dock, Swansea, in the early 1920s.

114. The coasting schooner *Kathleen & May* at Weaver's Basin in 1955. Launched in 1900 at Connah's Quay by Ferguson & Baird as a topsail schooner, she was later converted to fore-and-aft rigging and continued to trade until 1960, the last British sailing vessel to do so. She is now preserved as a museum ship at Plymouth.

115. The *Grace Hawar*, berthed at Prince of Wales Dock, loading coal in October 1929. Note in the background the newly built housing at Grenfell Park, St. Thomas.

116. Brixham Smacks sailing in Swansea Bay off Mumbles in 1920.

117. The paddle steamer *Glen Gower* leaves Swansea on an excursion trip in 1924. Probable destination - Ilfracombe.

118. The Blue Funnel Line Cargo Liner the SS *Ulysses* at A Shed, King's Dock, in September 1930. She weighed 14,501 tons gross and was built at Belfast in 1913.

119. The 'Banana Fleet' at Swansea Docks. Four Elder & Fyffe cargo liners bunkering at King's Dock in 1932.

120. The *British Pride* and the *City of Canberra* at King's Dock in June 1947.

121. The *City of Canberra* loading general cargo bound for South East Africa at No 3 Quay, King's Dock.

WEAVER & COMPANY LIMITED

122. opposite page: Aerial view of North Dock in 1930 showing the old New Cut Bridge across the River Tawe, Weaver's Basin and Beaufort Dock.

123. this page: Swansea Docks in the late 1940s with St Thomas and Port Tennant in the background.

124. HMS *Zambesi* seen at the Prince of Wales Dock in July 1946. Launched in 1943, she was broken up at Briton Ferry in 1959. In the background is the French frigate *La Surprise*.

125. HMS *Anson*, a 'King George V' Class battleship, seen anchored in Swansea Bay in August 1947 whilst on a courtesy visit. With a displacement of 35,000 tons she was too big to enter the port. Built by Swan Hunter on the Tyne and launched in February 1940 *Anson* boasted ten 14 inch guns, sixteen 5.25 inch dual purpose guns and forty-eight 2 pdr AA pom-poms and a crew of 1,555 officers and men (increased to over 2,000 in wartime).

126. HMS *Solebay*, a Battle Class destroyer, pictured at Swansea Docks in November 1949. These very large destroyers were optimised for service in the Pacific with long range and powerful armament especially in the anti-aircraft role, and served until the comparatively recent past.

127. Ford Prefect and Anglia motor-cars await shipment to Portugal in M shed, King's Dock, April 1947.

128. Standard Vanguard and Austin of England motor-cars in A Transit Shed prior to being exported to Australia in September 1949.

129. The MV *City of Swansea* was built in Glasgow for the Ellerman Line in 1946, and in the photograph is seen loading for her maiden voyage at Swansea Docks. She displaced 9,900 tons gross. Note Swansea did not become a city until December 1969! A plaque presented to MV *City of Swansea* in 1946 was retrieved from the vessel before she was broken up in Taiwan in the late 1960s and is now displayed in Swansea's Industrial and Maritime Museum.

Evening Post

No. 24,215   FRIDAY, FEBRUARY 2, 1951   THREE-HALFPENCE

ballito Stockings

TOWN FINAL

BRAINS BEERS

SWANSEA DOCK DISASTER

Explosion wrecks big oil tanker
7 MEN KILLED: 7 IN HOSPITAL: 24 ESCAPE

Six firemen taken to hospital after a later explosion

FIVE bodies had been recovered this afternoon from the wreckage inside the empty tanker Atlantic Duchess, 12,000 tons, registered in Liberia and now in the Queen's Dock, Swansea, caused by a double explosion and fire early to-day, and a smaller explosion later, the causes of which have not yet been ascertained. Two more men were missing, and it was believed that they were dead inside the ship. Seven more, including the captain and a relief captain, are in the General Hospital, and 24 other survivors are at the Sailors'

STRICKEN VESSEL AFTER THE EXPLOSIONS

THE ATLANTIC DUCHESS—a picture taken as she was soon after dawn this morning. Smoke pours from the captain's brid Her back is broken amidships, and firemen play their hoses into her from the dockside. Below: A close-up of the dama

131. The tanker *Eiho Maru* was the first Japanese vessel to visit Swansea for twelve years when she berthed at Queen's Dock in April 1952. Built in 1951 she displaced 11,960 tons gross.

132. Lightships at the Trinity House Depot in King's Dock. January 1952.

133. Swansea Pilot Cutter, *Roger Beck*, served from 1925 to 1959.

134. A fifty ton floating crane, manoeuvred by tugs, loads a cargo of railway wagons bound for West Africa.

135. The Duke of Edinburgh Dry Dock nearing completion. It was finally opened in 1959 as the largest privately owned dry dock in the Bristol Channel.

136. The MV *Surrey* (8,227 tons gross) owned by the Federal Steam Navigation Co alongside at D shed, King's Dock in September 1962. Note at left the sleek shape of the Jaguar XK 140, one of the great British sports car designs of the postwar period.

137 & 138. *above*: The British India Line's educational cruise ship *Devonia* leaving King's Dock in May, 1966, assisted by the Diesel Tug *Cambrian*. Built in Glasgow and completed in 1939 the *Devonia* had an active wartime career as a troopship. *left*: The educational cruise ship *Nevasa* leaving Swansea Docks in 1967. A former troopship, the *Nevasa* was one of the finest of its type when built in 1956. She displaced 20,527 tons gross. The steam tug *Canning* is now preserved in the South Dock at Swansea Marina as part of the Industrial and Maritime Museum as an outside floating exhibit.

139 - 141. Cranes and boats but no planes.

142. HMS *Glamorgan*, a County Class guided-missile destroyer, on a visit to Swansea. The term destroyer is a misnomer when applied to vessels such as these, as they are comparable in size to many prewar cruisers. *Glamorgan* was modernized to carry four single Mk 50 MM38 Exocet SSM launchers (no reloads) in place of one of their two twin 4.5 inch gun mounts. During the Falklands War in 1982 *Glamorgan* survived a direct hit from a land launched MM38 Exocet, being the sixteenth, and last, British warship to be damaged by enemy action.

143. During the Second World War the light cruiser HMS *Arethusa* was adopted by the people of Swansea. *Arethusa* took part in the naval bombardment of the Normandy beaches on D-Day, 6 June 1944, shelling the German coastal battery at Le Mont. The modern day HMS *Arethusa* (F38), a Type 12 'Modified Leander' Class Frigate, completed in 1965, is seen visiting the Port of Swansea in 1986. During a major refit in 1977 the twin Mk 6 4.5 inch gun mounting was replaced by a GWS 40 Ikara ASW missile installation.

144 & 145. The latest Swansea-Cork Ferry is the *Celtic Pride*.

Mumbles Lifeboat

146 & 147. Not every vessel makes it safely into harbour. The following photographs are a tribute to the undoubted skill, courage and determination of those who man the Mumbles Lifeboat Station and their RAF and RN colleagues in the Air Sea Rescue service. On 23 April 1947 the *Samtampa* (*right*), a 7,000 ton vessel, was dashed to pieces in a 70mph hurricane on the Sker Rocks off Porthcawl, and all thirty-nine on board were lost. The Mumbles lifeboat (*pictured below*) was launched in the teeth of the storm and in trying to effect a desperate rescue, itself succumbed to the elements. All eight men of the crew lost their lives - the Mumbles lifeboat's third terrible disaster.

148. In honour of the Coxswain who died during the *Samtampa* rescue attempt, a lifeboat was named *William Gammon*. Coxswain Gammon had previously earned the RNLI's highest award for bravery, the Gold Medal, in 1944.

149. The Royal National Lifeboat Institution's Mumbles Station has earned one of the finest records in Britain for heroism and service since it was first established in 1835. Here we see the RNLB *Pentland* on training exercises in the 1980s.

150 & 151. Westland Sea King helicopter from RAF Brawdy landed at King George V playing fields, Ashleigh Road, to demonstrate its ability to rush survivors of incidents at sea to Singleton Hospital, May 1983.

152 & 153. Testing of the slipway at Mumbles Lifeboat Station with a new type of trials lifeboat. *below*: RNLB *Ethel Anne Measures*, the new Mumbles lifeboat put into service in 1987, here seen on exercise with RAF Sea King and Wessex SAR helicopters.

Industry

154. The Lower Swansea Valley Project was started in 1967 to reclaim and improve the largest single area of industrial dereliction in Britain. New industries are being actively encouraged to set up business in the area to replace the traditional industries of metal-working and coal mining which have slowly declined over the course of this century.

155. The Tir John Power Station, which was built during the Depression Years to ease the unemployment situation in the Swansea area, and which burned anthracite coal hewn from the North West Coalfield, was finally demolished in the early 1980s.

156. The derelict Duffryn Steel and Tinplate Works at Morriston.

157. By 1961, 60% of the Lower Swansea Valley was in a derelict condition. Some seven million tons of slag heaps, ruined factory buildings and abandoned works, disused railway lines and polluted canals littered over 800 acres of the Tawe Valley. Much of the topsoil was so poisoned that nothing could grow.

158. The disused Weaver & Co Mill at North Dock Basin, reputedly the first concrete building in the world, was pulled down in the early 1980s.

159. opposite page: Brynlliw Colliery near Gorseinon, the last working coal mine in the Swansea area, was closed in 1983.

160. BP tank farm on Crymlyn Burrows, Swansea. Queen's Dock was opened as an oil terminal in 1920 to serve the Anglo-Persian Oil Co's new refinery at Llandarcy (which opened in 1922).

161 & 162. *above*: BP fireboat for use in the docks. *left*: BP tanker *British Crusader*.

164 & 165. The sky at night is never dark over BP's Refinery at Llandarcy.

166 & 167. BP Llandarcy photographed from the air in July 1983. During the Second World War the Luftwaffe attempted to bomb the refinery on more than one occasion, setting it on fire on 10 July 1940 and again on the night of 1/2 September 1940 - the ruptured oil tanks took several days to burn themselves out.

168. Ford Motor Co's Axle and Commercial Transmission Plant at Jersey Marine is a major employer in the Swansea region.

169. The Aluminium Wire & Cable Co Ltd's Jersey Marine Works.

170. A study in contrasts. In the foreground is the Baglan Bay petro-chemical works and in the background is Mumbles Head, one of the loveliest landmarks on the Gower Peninsula.

171. Distillation columns on the ethylene plant of British Hydrocarbon Chemicals Ltd at Baglan Bay.

172. BP Baglan Bay - a city of metal tubes.

173. The largest three Ms plant in the UK is at Gorseinon near Swansea, which produces a wide range of self-adhesive, printed, magnetic computer and video tapes. With a size of 600,000 square feet three Ms (Minnesota Mining & Manufacturing Co Ltd) employs about 4,000 people in technical, production and quality control work.

174. British Steel, Port Talbot, photographed in the early 1980s - at one time the largest integrated iron and steel works in Europe.

175. Velindre Tinplate Works, with the M4 in the distance.

176 & 177. The Raw Materials Preparation Unit building of Morganite Carbon Ltd emphasises the clean, functional lines of the new factory at Morriston, Swansea. All functions within the building are fully automated and are operated from a central computerised control console. Morganite employs nearly 1,000 people in its factory which stands on the site of the old Upper Forest Works.

178. British Steel, Landore Works.

179. Aerial view of the Lower Swansea Valley showing the Beaufort Industrial Estate, British Steel at Landore and the Landore railway viaduct.

Leisure and Sport

180 - 183. The 1980s have seen an exciting new development at Swansea's old South Dock - the Maritime Quarter and Marina. The South Dock and Half Tide Basin have been reclaimed from a state of acute dereliction and turned into a recreational and residential area with the timely application of flair and imagination.

184. The Maritime and Industrial Museum, South Dock. Berthed alongside are the floating exhibits - the lightship *Helwick* and the Steam Tug *Canning*.

185. The old Pump House at South Dock has been tastefully converted into a restaurant, showing what can be done with old buildings of character and interest.

186 & 187. A good example of the architectural style of the new Maritime Quarter.

188 & 189. Small craft moored at the new berths on the River Tawe.

190. Windsurfing is a comparatively recent addition to the watersport scene.

191. Yachting in Swansea Bay off Mumbles Head, with Mumbles Lighthouse in the background.

192. In 1965 an inshore rescue boat station was established at Mumbles for rescues involving small pleasure boats or swimmers in difficulties fairly close to shore.

193 & 194. Seafishing in Swansea Bay at sunset - a tranquil scene . . . but you could end up with one of these on the end of the line. Shark! Help!

195. Funfair at Brynmill Recreation Ground, Summer 1987.

196. Miss Swansea beauty contest at the Patti Pavilion, August 1987.

197. A walk in Clyne Valley Country Park, 1986.

198. Swansea Flower Show, August 1987.

199. Aerial view of Oystermouth, with its mid-thirteenth century castle, and The Mumbles.

200 - 202. Mumbles Pier is an ideal spot for seafishing.

203. Small yachts and pleasure craft at Mumbles.

204 & 205. Mumbles Head with its distinctive landmark - the Lighthouse.

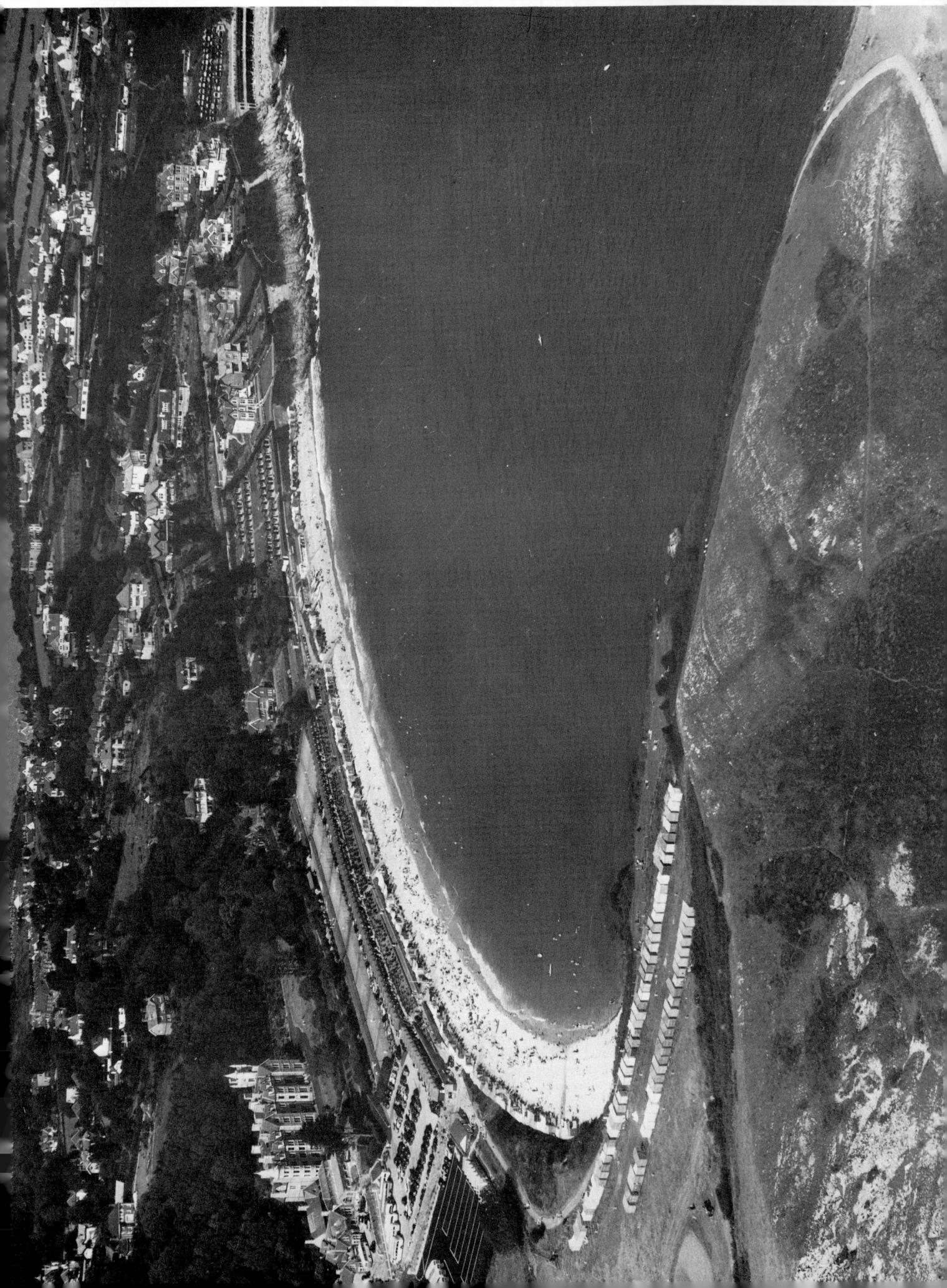

206. *opposite page:* Langland Bay at the height of summer, 1958.

207. *above:* Langland Bay, June 1986.

209. The Gower Show, August 1987.

210. Pennard Castle, Gower.

211 & 212. One of the most beautiful parts of the Gower Peninsula -
Three Cliffs Bay.

213. The view north from Rhossili

214. In 1957 the National Parks Commission designated Gower as an 'area of outstanding natural beauty', the first place in Britain to be so termed. This is a view of Worms Head and Rhossili Bay.

215. Hang-gliding from the top of Rhossili Down.

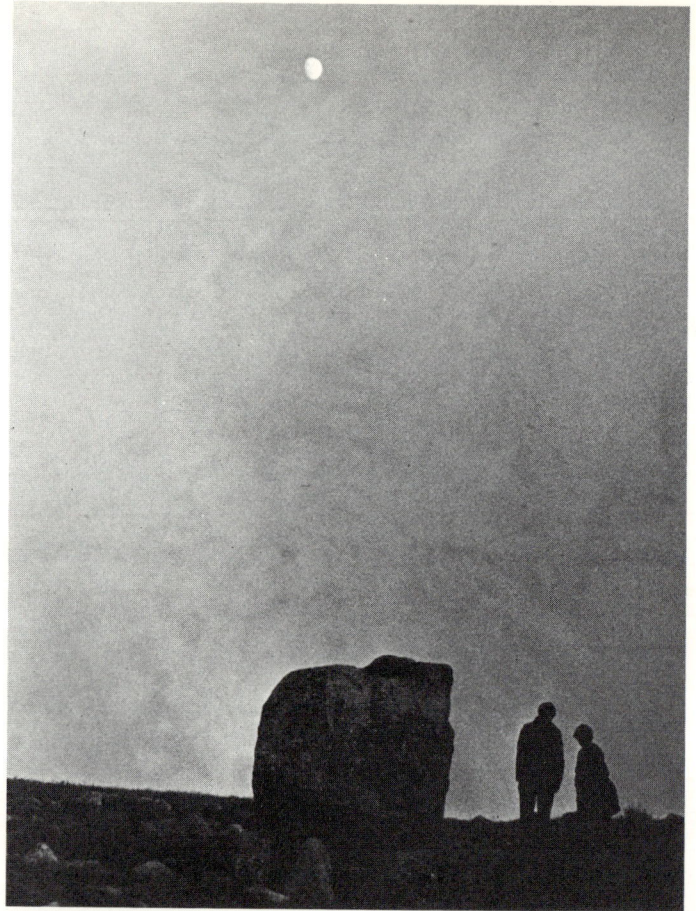

216. Arthur's Stone on top of Cefn Bryn, Gower, is a Neolithic burial chamber with a capstone weighing an estimated 25 tons. The legend is that King Arthur was one day walking in Carmarthenshire when he felt a pebble in his shoe. He threw it away and it landed on Cefn Bryn.

217. Cockle gatherers making their way home from far out on Llanrhidian Sands.

218. Can you see me mother?! Start of a 10km race, 1987.

219. Swansea City 6, Rhyl 1, January 1971.

220. Glory Days! John Toshack took The Swans to Division One in the early 1980s.

221. Arthur Emyr (Wing) scoring a try for The All Whites against Bristol at St Helen's Rugby Ground in September 1987.

222. St Helen's Cricket Ground is the nearest one in the country to the sea.

223. Don Shepherd holds a stump aloft to salute Glamorgan's victory over the Australians by seventy-nine runs, St Helen's, August 1968. Note Peter Walker between

224. Swansea Parachute Club is based at Fairwood aerodrome. These two girls have just trained to do a parachute jump for charity.

225. The long arm of the law. Police keeping an eye on things at Mumbles Carnival in July 1987.

226. Comic Relief, 5 February 1988.

Swansea Beach

227. This card was posted in September 1921 to an address in Birmingham. It reads "Having a lovely time and feeling much better for the change. Swansea and Mumbles are magnificent. Returning to Birmingham Monday. Weather perfect. Love from Agnes."

228. The Foreshore, September 1987.

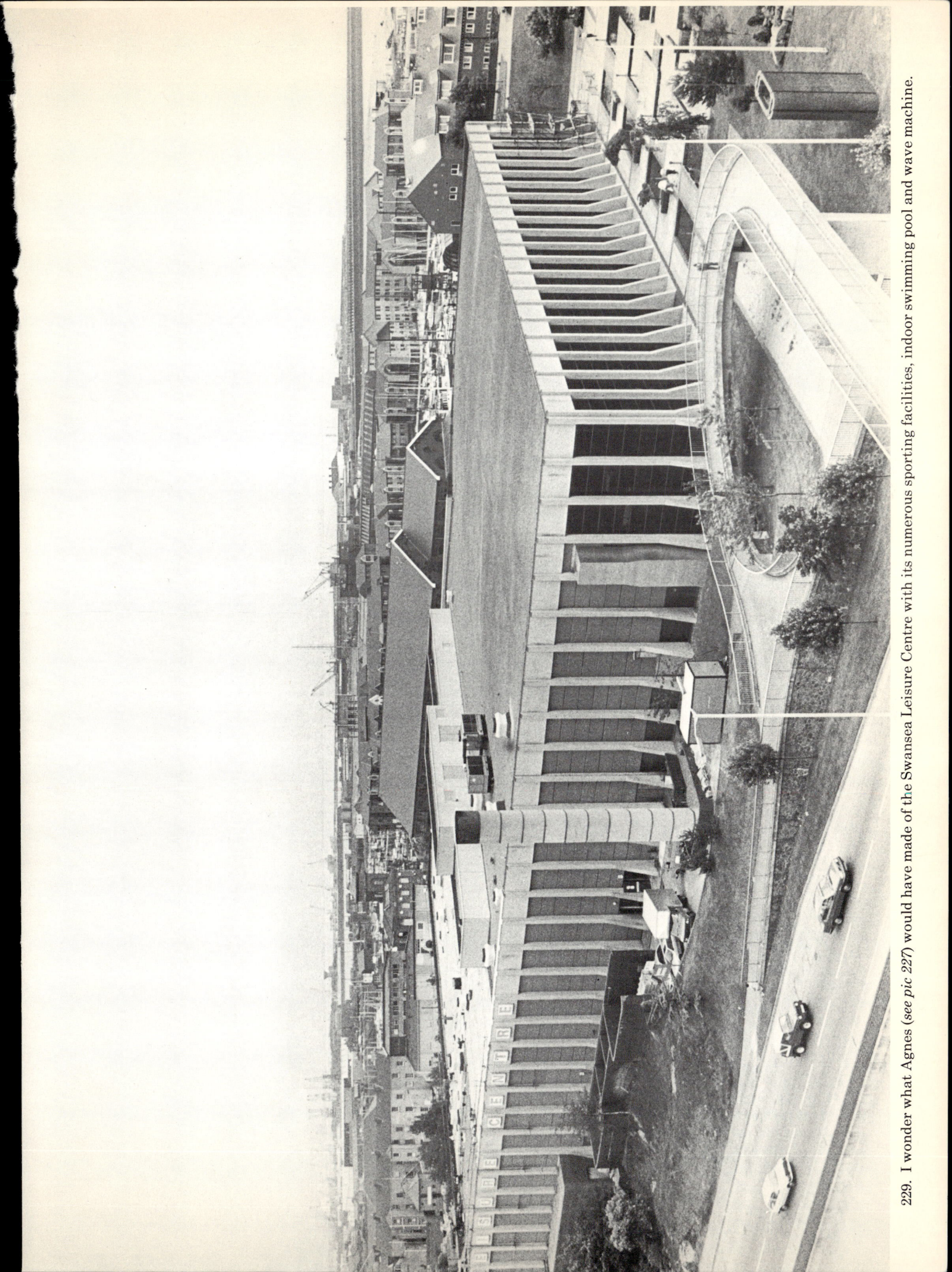

229. I wonder what Agnes (*see pic 227*) would have made of the Swansea Leisure Centre with its numerous sporting facilities, indoor swimming pool and wave machine.